AF584805

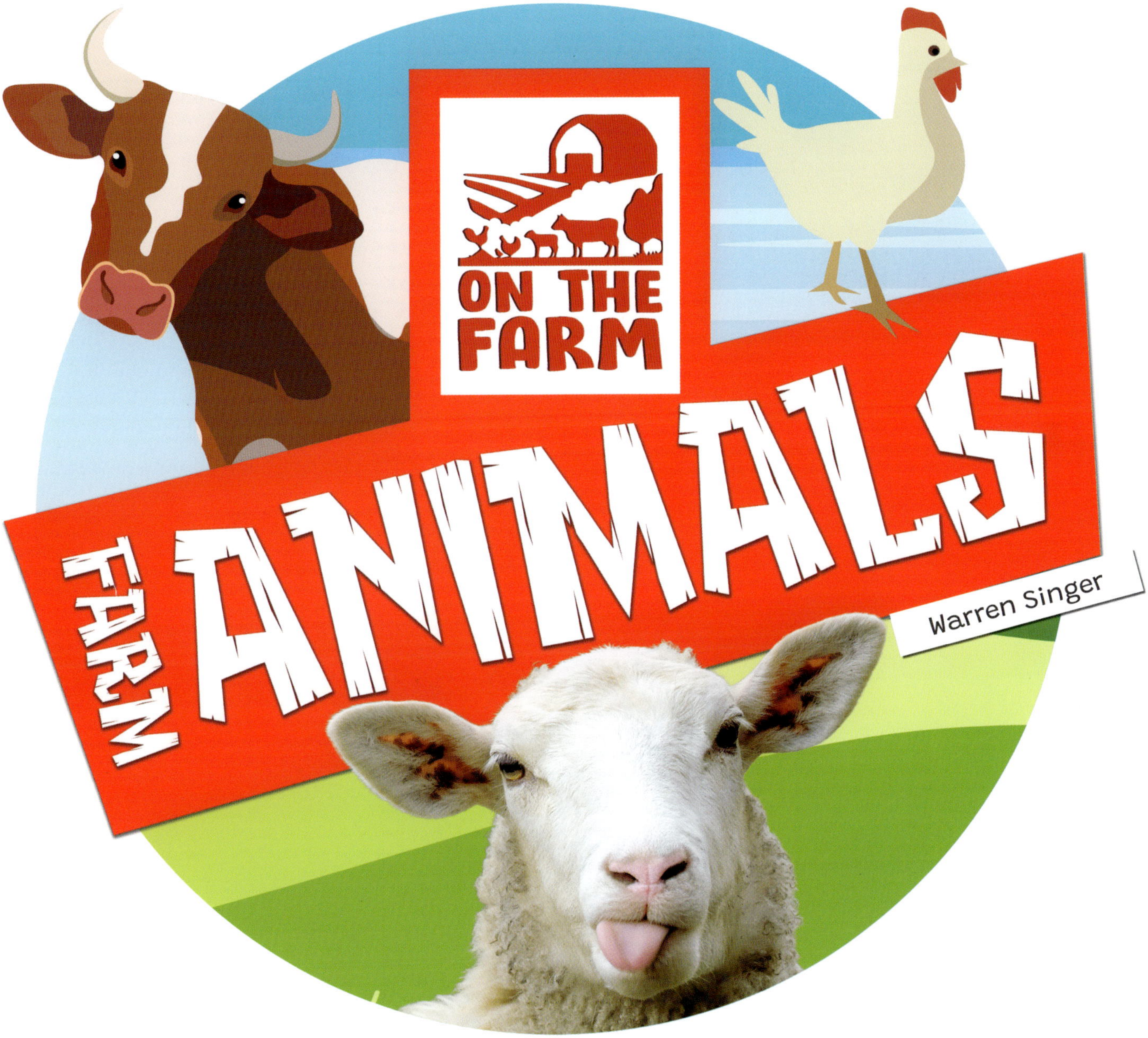

On the Farm

Farm Animals

Warren Singer

First Published 2025 by
Redback Publishing
Suite 6, 13a Narabang Way,
Belrose NSW 2085
Australia

www.redbackpublishing.com
orders@redbackpublishing.com

ISBN 978-1-761400-78-0

Author: Warren Singer
Editors: Lucinda Dodds and Emma Dobinson
Designer: Redback Publishing
Original illustrations © Redback Publishing 2025
Originated by Redback Publishing

Acknowledgements
Abbreviations: l—left, r—right, b—bottom, t—top, c—centre, m—middle
We would like to thank the following for permission to reproduce photographs: Shutterstock; p16l S1001 / Shutterstock.com, p20bl Bob Pool / Shutterstock.com

A catalogue record for this book is available from the National Library of Australia

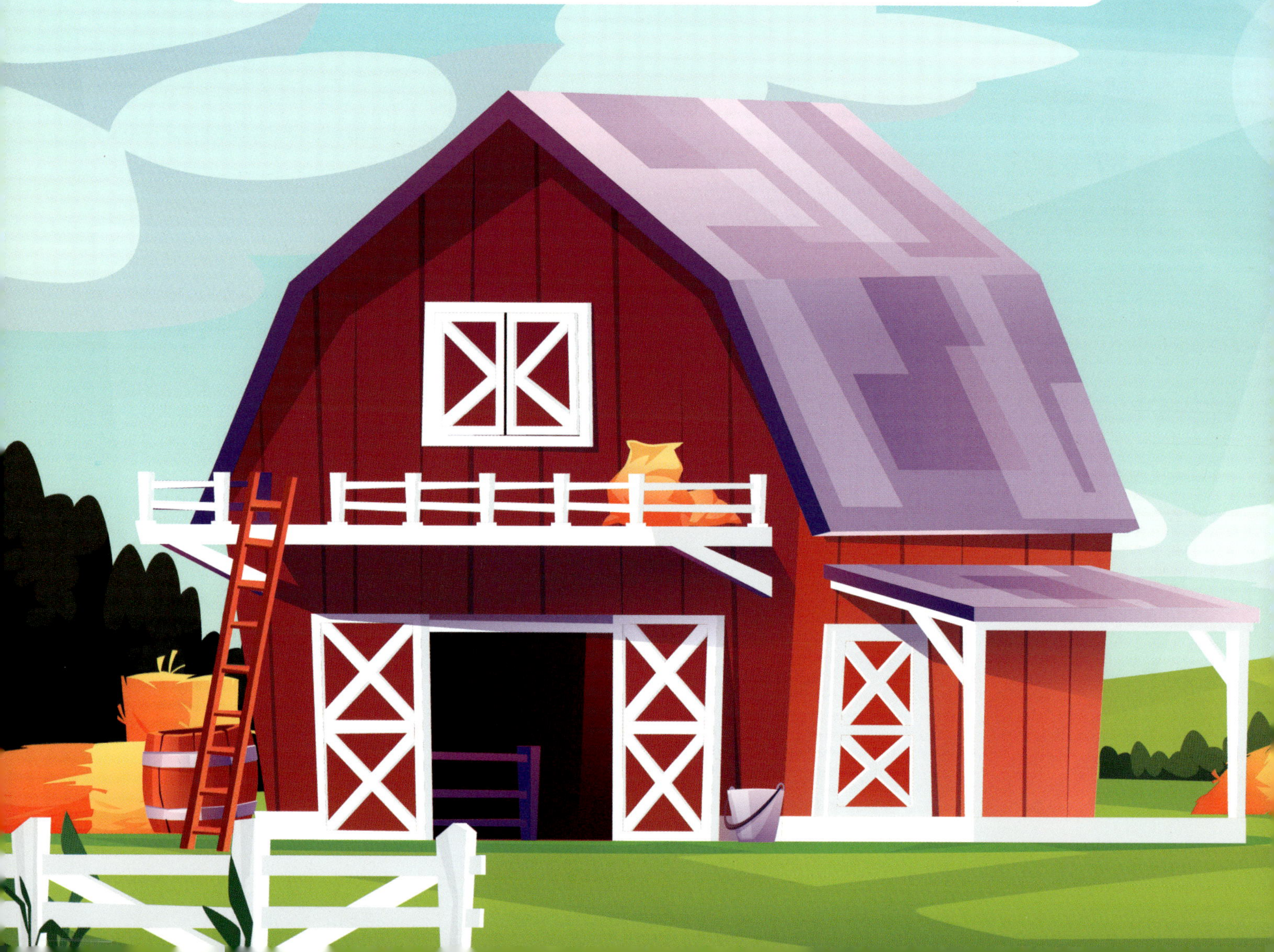

CONTENTS

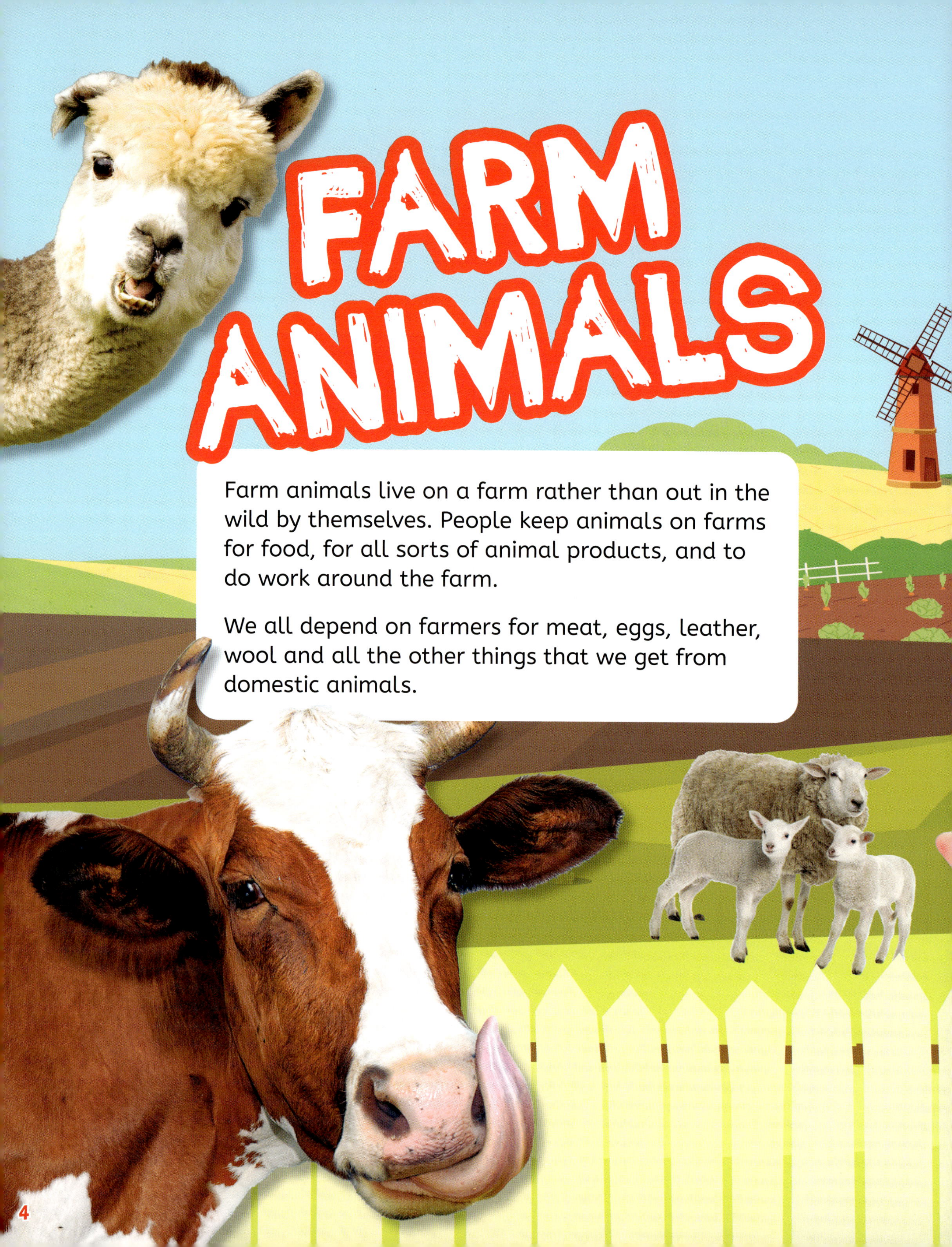

FARM ANIMALS

Farm animals live on a farm rather than out in the wild by themselves. People keep animals on farms for food, for all sorts of animal products, and to do work around the farm.

We all depend on farmers for meat, eggs, leather, wool and all the other things that we get from domestic animals.

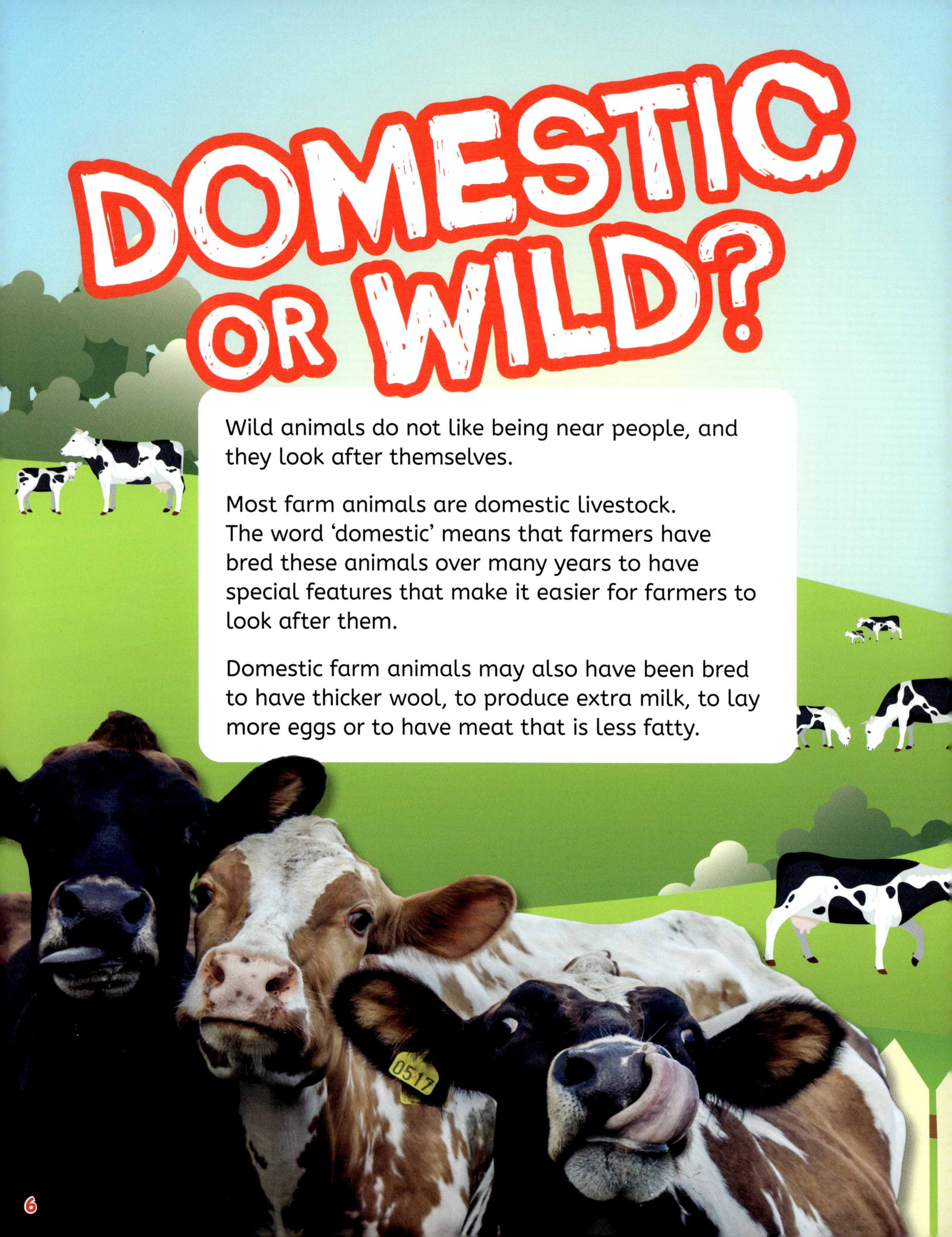

DOMESTIC OR WILD?

Wild animals do not like being near people, and they look after themselves.

Most farm animals are domestic livestock. The word 'domestic' means that farmers have bred these animals over many years to have special features that make it easier for farmers to look after them.

Domestic farm animals may also have been bred to have thicker wool, to produce extra milk, to lay more eggs or to have meat that is less fatty.

FACT
Domestic animals have all come from wild animals in the past.

FACT
Domestic cattle were first bred from wild aurochs.

PETS ON FARMS

DOGS

A working dog will keep the cattle or sheep together, stop some of them wandering off, and help the farmer to move them into yards.

CATS

Cats on farms help to keep rats and mice away. This is their job on the farm, they often like to come inside and sit with the family just like a pet cat does in the city.

FACT

Sometimes a working dog will also be the farmer's pet.

HORSES

On large farms around the world, horses are used to muster or herd the sheep and cattle. The horse and the rider develop a special bond, and the horse learns exactly what it needs to do when it is working on a farm.

FACT

Farm livestock are not pets. They are kept to provide income for the farmer.

BABY ANIMALS

Children on farms may have the job of looking after a sick baby lamb or calf, but it cannot be their pet forever.

WHAT FARM ANIMALS EAT

Even though cattle, sheep and goats eat grass in a field, farmers also give them extra vitamins and minerals to keep them healthy.

Hay is dried grass that farmers store and feed to their animals when there is not enough fresh grass.

On chicken farms, the chickens are usually fed special pellets that are mostly made of grains and some meat products.

FACT
Water is vital on farms. Without it a farm could not exist.
FACT
On fish farms, farmers feed the fish pellets made of grains and other fish.

VETS

Vets are doctors for animals. Farmers need vets to help keep the farm animals healthy.

Vets help farm animals to give birth to babies, they look after animals that have been injured, and they give them injections to prevent diseases.

Farmers may need a vet to look after a herd of hundreds of animals, or just one very large and heavy bull. These sorts of jobs have to be done on the farm and not in the vet's office or surgery.

FACT
Vets trim the hooves and horns of farm animals.

FACT
Vets test farm animals for diseases that could spread to people.

CARING FOR FARM ANIMALS

Looking after farm animals is hard work. A farmer cannot take a holiday and ignore the animals, as they need to be checked on and fed every day.

Like all living things, farm animals need shelter and protection. Farms have sheds, cages, barns, stables and fencing to protect the livestock.

Farmers keep their animals as healthy as possible so they can get the best price for them when they are sold.

FACT
Farmers need to learn basic first aid for animals.

Predators of farm animals include foxes, wolves, dingoes, eagles, wild pigs, pythons and feral cats and dogs.

FACT
Modern farmers need to know a lot about science.

DID YOU KNOW?
Farmers often start working before the sun comes up.

GOING TO MARKET

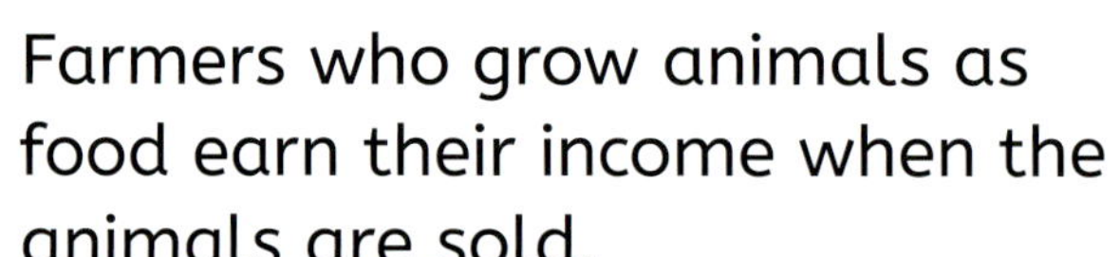

Farmers who grow animals as food earn their income when the animals are sold.

You will sometimes see huge trucks full of farm animals on their way to market. Animals, or their meat, are also transported overseas in ships feeding people far away from where the food was grown.

Vegetarians choose not to eat meat.

FACT

'Going to market' means that an animal is sent away to be turned into food for people.

FACT

Humans have been eating meat from farm animals for many thousands of years.

DID YOU KNOW?

The largest livestock ship can transport 75,000 sheep or 18,000 cattle around the globe.

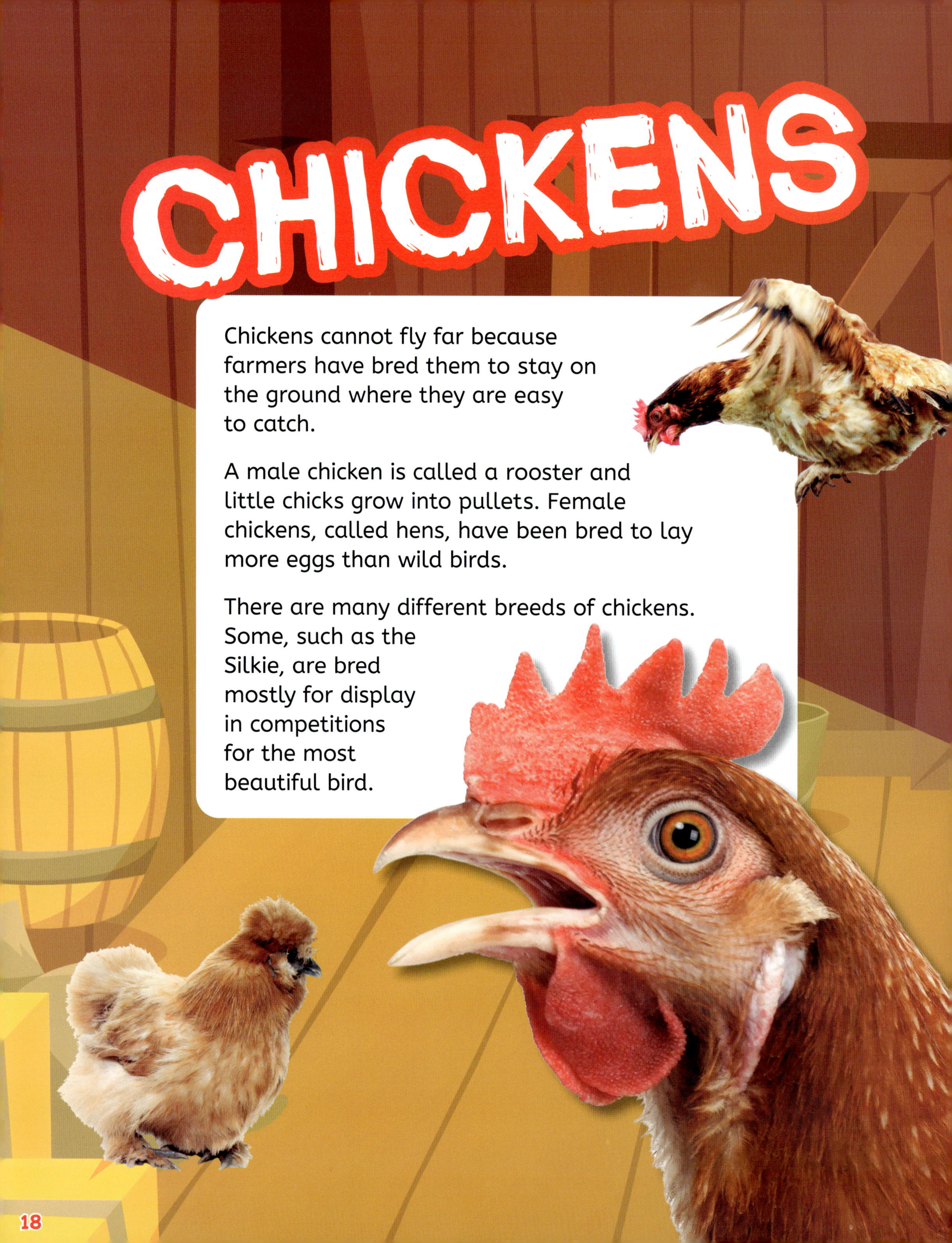

CHICKENS

Chickens cannot fly far because farmers have bred them to stay on the ground where they are easy to catch.

A male chicken is called a rooster and little chicks grow into pullets. Female chickens, called hens, have been bred to lay more eggs than wild birds.

There are many different breeds of chickens. Some, such as the Silkie, are bred mostly for display in competitions for the most beautiful bird.

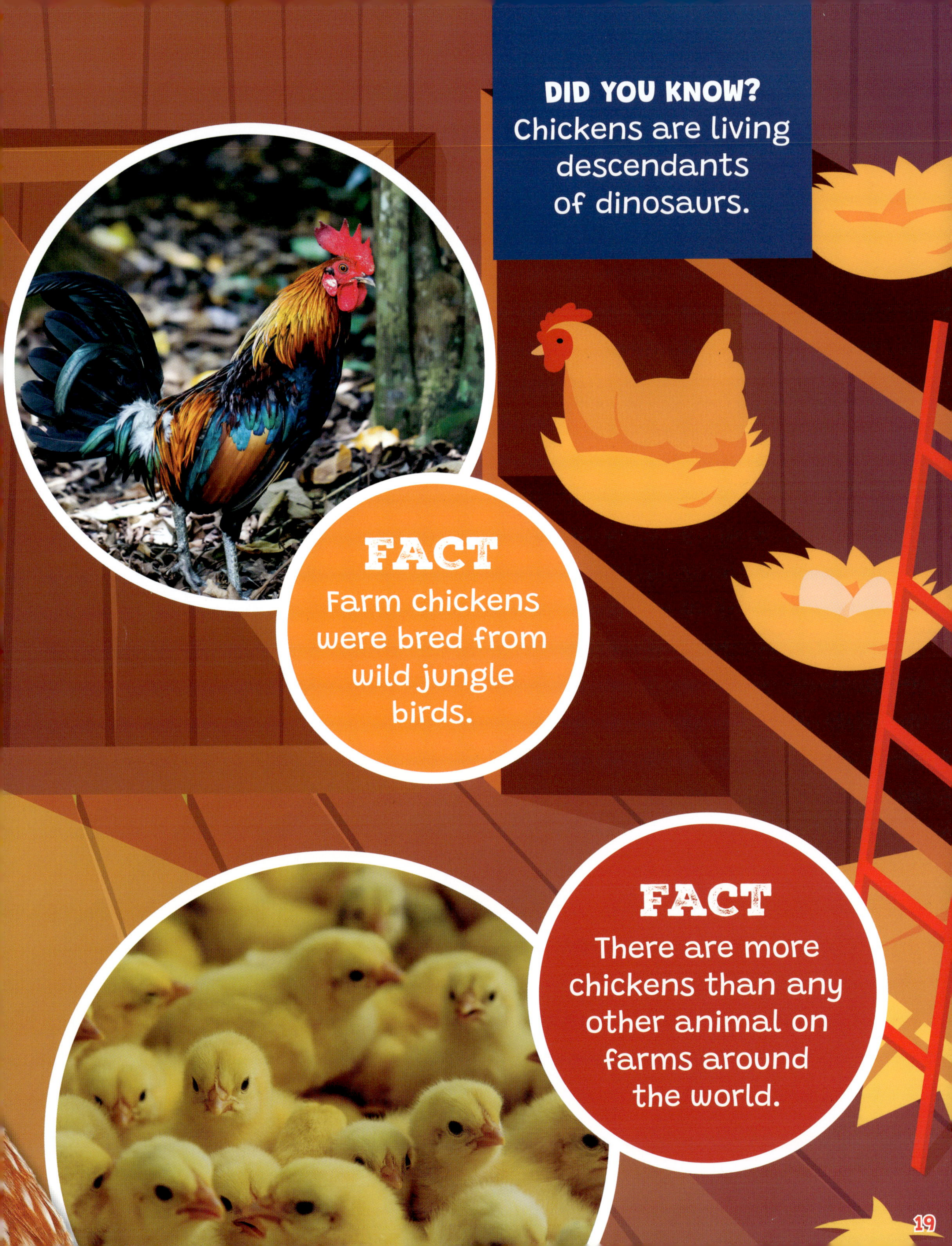
DID YOU KNOW?
Chickens are living descendants of dinosaurs.
FACT
Farm chickens were bred from wild jungle birds.
FACT
There are more chickens than any other animal on farms around the world.

Herds of beef cattle and dairy cows require large areas of land for food and lots of fresh water.

Some very large farms can be bigger than countries, and are known as stations or ranches. Farm hands called 'stockmen' or 'cowboys' look after the cattle, and herd them to fresh pastures.

Cows in a dairy herd are all female, they are raised to produce milk.

FACT

The USA has more beef cattle than any other country.

FACT

Methane emissions from cows contribute to global warming and climate change.

DID YOU KNOW?
Cows have no upper front teeth.

PIGS

Pigs are farmed mainly for food such as bacon, ham, pork chops, and sausages. Some pigskin is used for leather.

Compared to other livestock pigs can grow very quickly when provided with a consistent supply of grains, pig feed and fresh water.

Farmers have to be careful that their pigs do not carry diseases or worms that could infect humans who eat the meat.

FACT
Pigs are very intelligent, and may be as smart as dogs.

FACT
Wild pigs are very dangerous animals.

DID YOU KNOW?
Newborn piglets learn to run to the sound of their mother's voice.

Goats are kept on farms to provide meat, milk and skins.

A herd of goats does not need as much land as a herd of cattle, they are much easier for farmers to look after.

Farmers need to ensure their goats are securely fenced in as goats can easily climb trees where they like to eat the leaves. This also means they can get out of a farmyard by climbing the fences.

Angora goats have very soft hair that people knit or weave into clothes and blankets.

FACT
Goat farming started over 10,000 years ago.

FACT
A baby goat is called a kid, a female is a nanny, and a male is a billy.

DID YOU KNOW?
Goats have rectangular pupils.

SHEEP

Sheep are farmed for their wool which is turned into clothes and blankets to keep people warm, and their milk is made into cheese and yoghurt.

Sheep like to stay together in a large group, called a flock or mob. This makes it easier for farmers to move them around the farm to graze on grass and plants. Farmers will feed them extra hay or grains to keep them in good condition.

FACT

Feta and ricotta cheese are made from sheep's milk.

FACT

A baby sheep is called a lamb, a female is a ewe, and male is a ram.

DID YOU KNOW?

453 grams (one pound) of wool can make up to 16 kilometres (10 miles) of thread.

Horses are very helpful on farms. These beautiful strong animals are used to muster livestock, to pull carts, and for riding.

They need metal horseshoes attached to their hooves to protect their feet from injury.

Farms where horses are bred for racing are called stud farms.

FACT
A baby horse is called a foal, a female is a mare, and a male is a stallion.

FACT
A horse will often form a strong friendship with another animal in its stable or paddock.

DID YOU KNOW?
A horse can sleep standing up.

UNUSUAL FARM ANIMALS

RATS

People farm rats to be sold as food for pet snakes.

INSECTS

Insects such as crickets and moths are raised on farms for humans and animals to eat.

OSTRICHES

The ostrich is the biggest bird in the world. It is farmed for its feathers and meat.

ALPACAS

Alpacas produce a soft wool that can be made into clothes.

GLOSSARY

calf .... baby cow or bull

domestic .... being an animal that is bred and kept by people

hay .... dried grass used as food for animals

herd .... group of cattle

lamb .... baby sheep

livestock .... animals on a farm

mob .... a large group of sheep

muster .... gather animals together

pellets .... small, hard balls

python .... big snake

ranch .... cattle farm in the USA

stable .... building to house horses or other animals

INDEX